MW01675919

Great Piano

THE MINI SERIES

GEORGE FRIDERIC HANDEL

Compiled and Edited by DALE TUCKER

CONTENTS

WARNER BROS. PUBLICATIONS - THE GLOBAL LEADER IN PRINT
USA: 15800 NW 48th Avenue, Miami, FL 33014

WARNER/CHAPPELL MUSIC
CANADA: 85 SCARSDALE ROAD, SUITE 101
DON MILLS, ONTARIO, M3B 2R2
SCANDINAVIA: P.O. BOX 533, VENDEVAGEN 85 B
S-182 15, DANDERYD, SWEDEN
AUSTRALIA: P.O. BOX 353
3 TALAVERA ROAD, NORTH RYDE N.S.W. 2113

NUOVA CARISCH
ITALY: VIA CAMPANIA, 12
20098 S. GIULIANO MILANESE (MI)
ZONA INDUSTRIALE SESTO ULTERIANO
SPAIN: MAGALLANES, 25
28015 MADRID
FRANCE: 25 RUE DE HAUTEVILLE, 75010 PARIS

INTERNATIONAL MUSIC PUBLICATIONS LIMITED
ENGLAND: SOUTHEND ROAD,
WOODFORD GREEN, ESSEX IG8 8HN
GERMANY: MARSTALLSTR. 8, D-80539 MUNCHEN
DENMARK: DANMUSIK, VOGNMAGERGADE 7
DK 1120 KOBENHAVNK

GEORGE FREDERIC HANDEL

Born: February 23, 1685-Halle, Germany
Died: April 14, 1759-London, England

Georg Friedrich Händel (original spelling) was born in Halle, Germany on February 23, 1685 to a minister's daughter and a sixty-three year old father who served as court surgeon to the Duke of Saxe-Weissenfels. On a visit to the court, as he often did, Handel played the organ, and was heard by the Duke who persuaded Handel's father to send him to study. Handel became a student of Wilhelm Zachau, later substituted for him at the church, and contributed musical compositions to the service. In 1702 Handel entered the University in Halle and took the position of organist there. During the year 1703, he traveled to Hamburg to work with Reinhard Keiser, the composer/director of the Hamburg Opera. While there, Handel met Johann Mattheson, and the two traveled to Lubeck to apply for the position of organist vacated by the death of Buxtehude. Neither took the post.

Around this time, Handel began composing operas, and continued to travel. In 1706 he went to Italy, where he stayed for six years, and met Allessandro and Domenico Scarlatti. He composed many operas there before returning to Germany in 1710 to take the post of Kapellmeister to the Elector of Hanover. In 1713 Handel composed a choral work in honor of Queen Anne's birthday, which won him favor with the royal family. Upon the death of Queen Anne in 1714, the Elector of Hanover became King George I of England, and Handel was brought to England at an increased salary. He eventually became a British subject and changed the spelling of his name to that used today. Under King George I, more operas were composed and performed as well as one of his famous instrumental works, *Water Music*.

Prosperous years followed with involvement in the Royal Academy of Music, the King's Theatre, and anthems composed for the Duke of Chandos and the coronation of King George II. Handel's output of operas continued, and in 1734 he established his own company at Covent Garden. None of his operas survived, with performances dwindling during his lifetime, which led him to the composition of oratorios, including his masterpiece, *Messiah,* which was written and orchestrated in less than one month.

Although Handel and J.S. Bach were born and lived at the same time, they never met. Musically, the two were very different with Bach concentrating on sacred works for church and instrumental music for study, while Handel traveled often and composed for the stage. Therefore, Handel was a popular figure in his lifetime, while Bach was known by few. Handel was a very religious man, as was Bach, but he never married.

In 1737 Handel suffered a stroke, and another in the 1740's, followed by failing eyesight in the early 1750's, all affecting his ability to compose, perform and conduct. His final public appearance was for a performance of the *Messiah* in 1759, and he died a few days later, on April 14th at his home on Brooke Street in London, a house which still stands today. His funeral was held at Westminster Abbey, where he is buried. Unlike many composers, Handel had a sizable estate at his death, the bulk of which was left to a niece in Germany, and the remainder distributed to friends and charities.

Handel's musical output was enormous, consisting of thirty-two volumes of operas, twenty-one of oratorios, seven of serenatas, twelve of sacred music, eleven of cantatas and five of instrumental music.

SONATINA

GEORGE FRIDERIC HANDEL

SARABANDE

from *Suite No. 6*

1) 

GAVOTTE AND VARIATIONS

from *Suite No. 14*

1) 

Variation I

Variation IV

GIGUE IN B FLAT MAJOR

from *Suite No. 13*

p
f
p
mf
poco rit.

TWO MINUETS IN F MAJOR

No. 1

Allegretto con moto

1) 

No. 2

Allegretto con moto

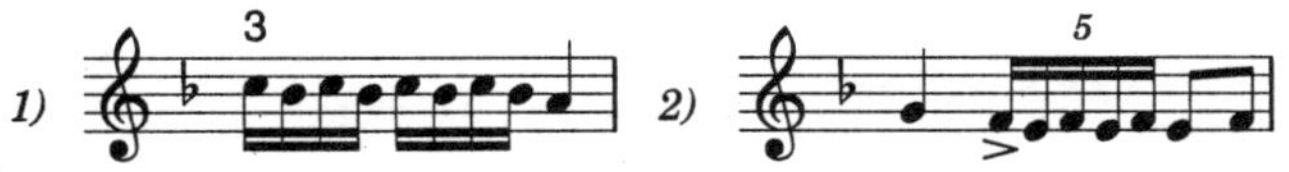

COURANTE

from *Suite No. 14*

1) 

SARABANDE

from *Suite No. 4*

Moderato

1) 

1) 

PRELUDE IN G MAJOR

SARABANDE

from *Suite No. 11*

Grave

Variation I

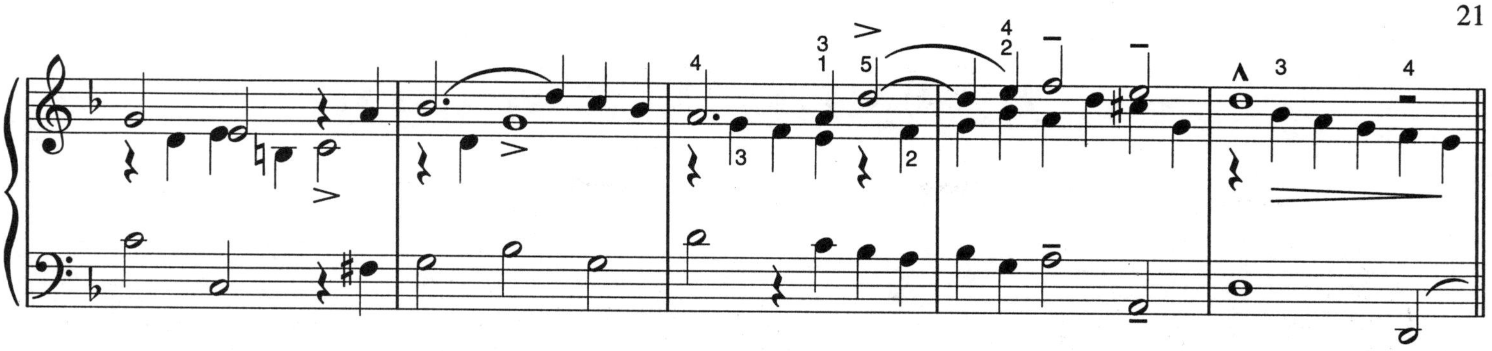

Variation II

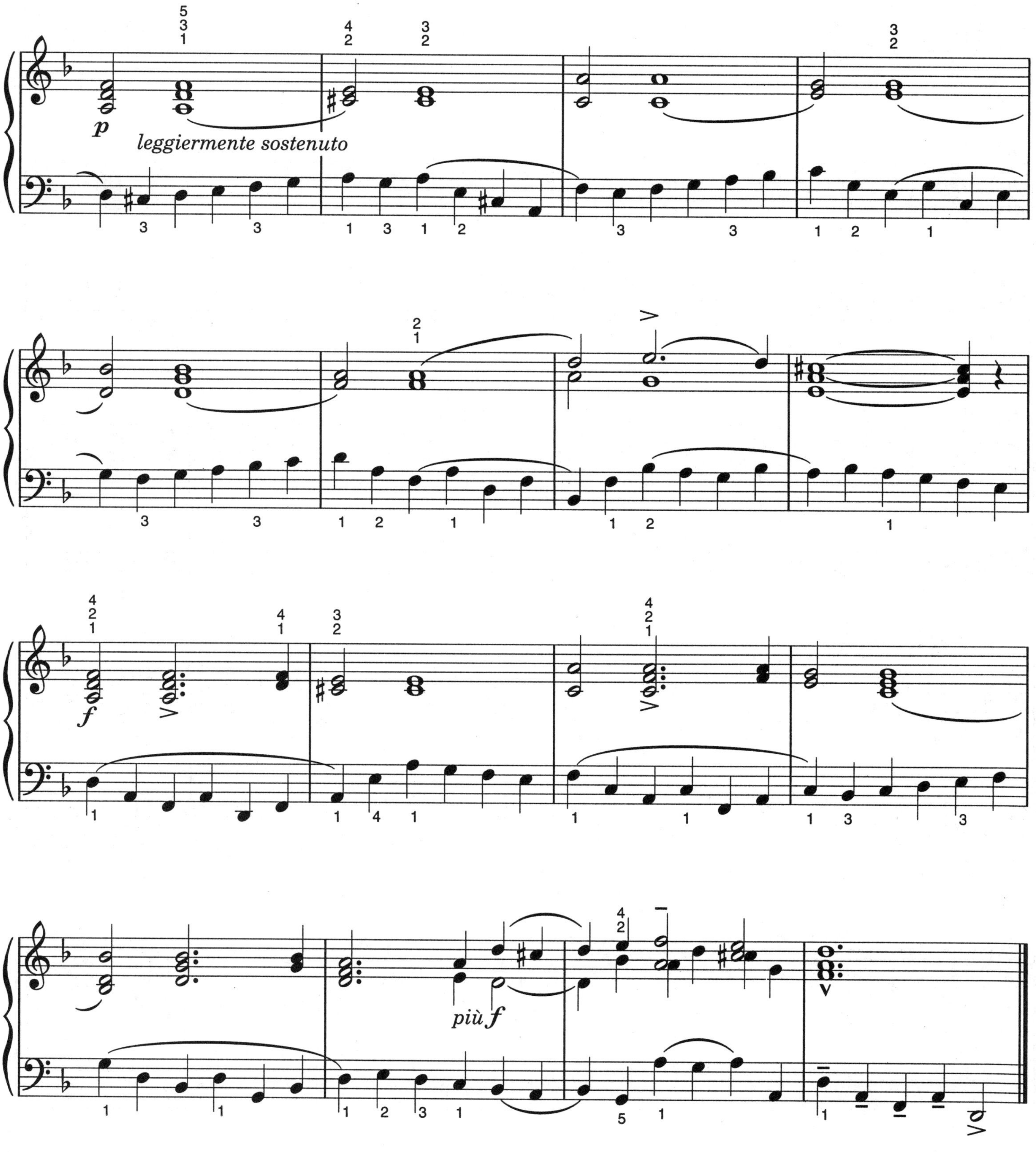

SARABANDE IN F MAJOR

ALLEGRO

from *Suite No. 6*

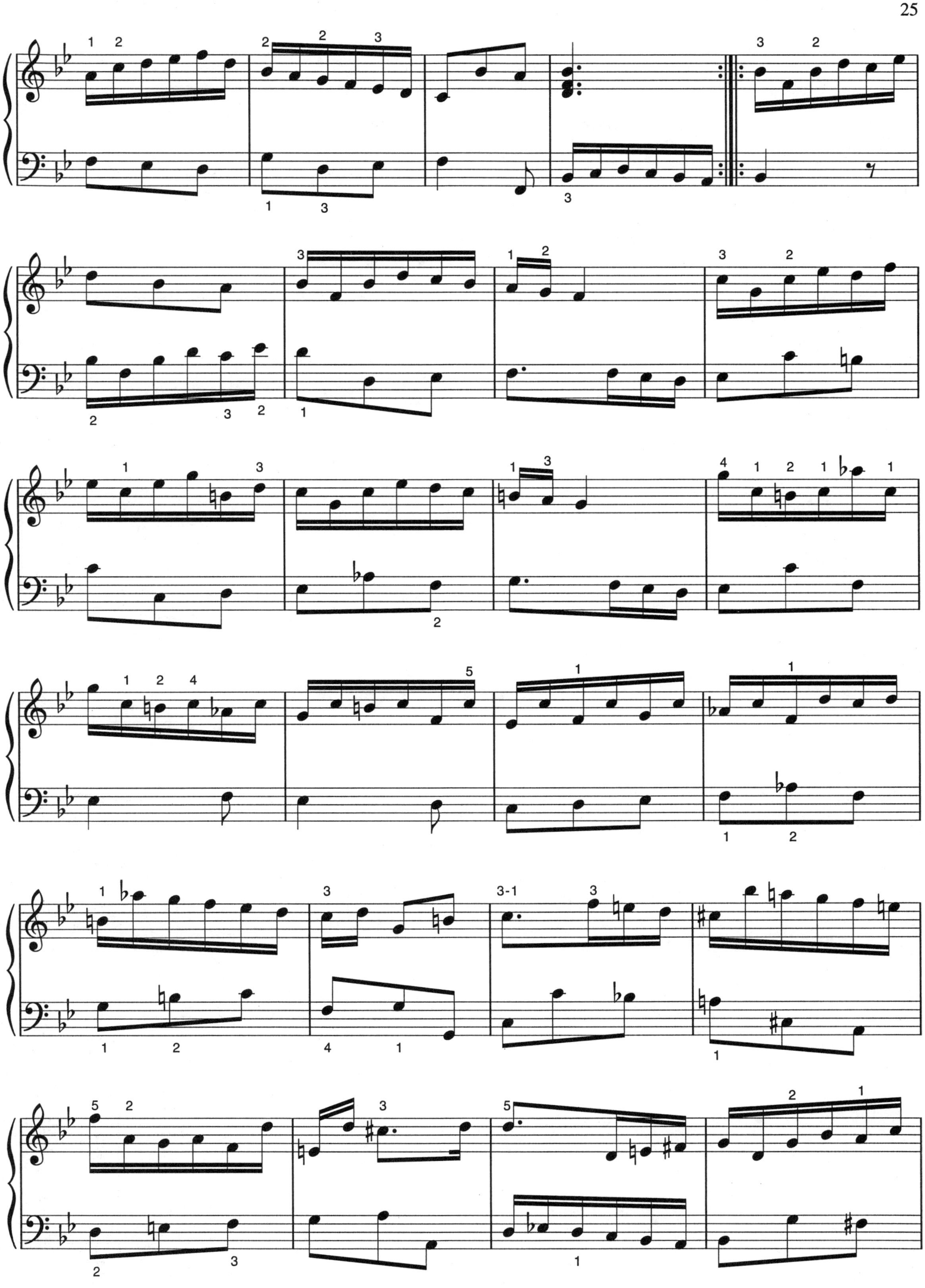

GIGUE

from *Suite No. 14*

Vivace

p
p
f

ALLEMANDE

from *Suite No. 16*

cresc.
f
1)